How to use this book

Matched to the National Curriculum, this Collins Year 2 Spelling workbook is designed to improve spelling skills.

Handy **tips** included throughout.

Questions split into three levels of difficulty – **Challenge 1**, **Challenge 2** and **Challenge 3** – to help progression.

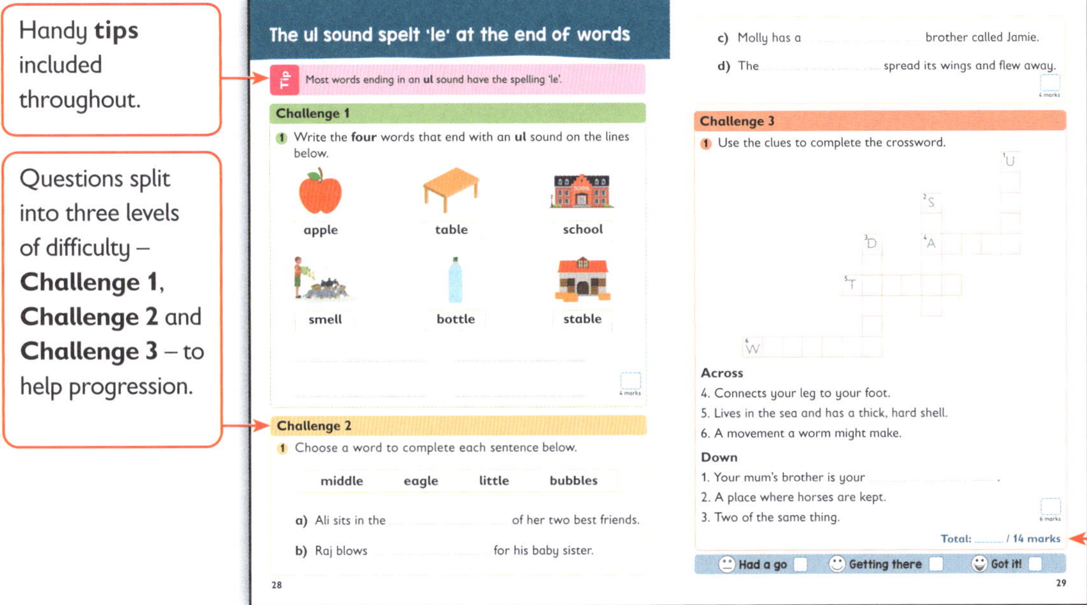

Teaching notes to guide you through some of the key aspects of spelling.

Total marks boxes for recording progress and **'How am I doing?'** checks for self-evaluation.

Starter test recaps skills covered in Year 1.

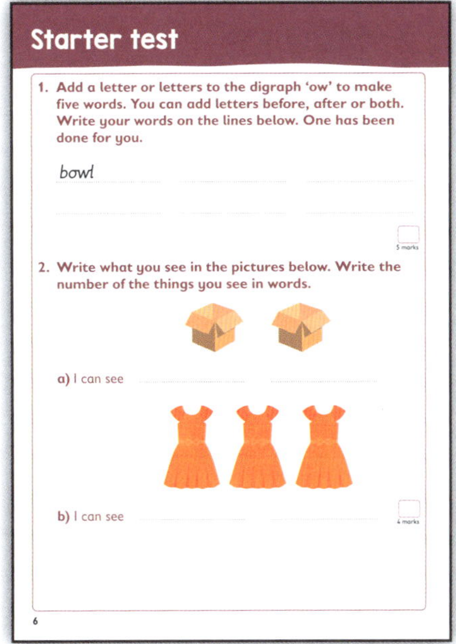

Four **Progress tests** included throughout the book for ongoing assessment and monitoring progress.

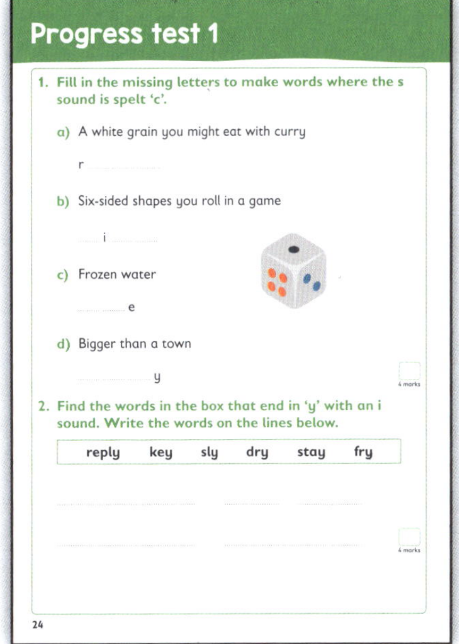

Answers provided for all the questions.

Contents

Acknowledgements

The author and publisher are grateful to the copyright holders for permission to use quoted materials and images.

All illustrations and images are ©Shutterstock.com and ©HarperCollins*Publishers* Ltd.

Published by Collins
An imprint of HarperCollins*Publishers*
1 London Bridge Street
London SE1 9GF

HarperCollins*Publishers*
Macken House, 39/40 Mayor Street Upper,
Dublin 1, D01 C9W8, Ireland

ISBN 978-0-00-862709-6

First published 2024

10 9 8 7 6 5 4 3 2 1

British Library Cataloguing in Publication Data.

A CIP record of this book is available from the British Library.

Publisher: Jennifer Hall
Author: Shelley Welsh
Project Leaders: Richard Toms and Shelley Teasdale
Editorial: Fiona Watson
Cover Design: Sarah Duxbury
Inside Concept Design and Page Layout: Ian Wrigley
Production: Emma Wood
Printed in India by Multivista Global Pvt. Ltd

This book is produced from independently certified FSC™ paper to ensure responsible forest management.

For more information visit: www.harpercollins.co.uk/green

Practising spelling at home

The systematic teaching of the sounds conveyed by letters and groups of letters is called phonics. In phonics teaching, children are shown how to spell a word by breaking it up into individual sounds, blending sounds and matching sounds to the letters of the alphabet. As part of phonics, children are taught about spelling patterns and spelling rules.

Developing the skill of blending sounds into words is important for reading familiar words, and is helpful when encountering new words.

In Year 2, children's writing ability tends to develop more slowly than their reading ability; this is because their spelling skills and physical handwriting skills are still developing, as well as the fact that they are still learning how to organise their ideas in writing.

Supporting your child

When supporting your child at home, draw their attention to spelling patterns. These might be sound or letter patterns, grammar patterns or word families. It is important to remember that although there are many spelling rules, there are also many words that are exceptions to any obvious rule or pattern. These words just have to be learned.

Your child's vocabulary can be extended by actively engaging in conversation with you and other adults, listening to you read to them from books, and reading independently. Encourage your child to be curious about vocabulary, its meaning and how it is spelt. Reading to and with your child, and discussing what has been read, will help your child develop their vocabulary and their understanding of grammar, as well as supporting their ability to access other areas of the curriculum.

There are many ways that your child can practise spelling at home, independently and with support, and there are a range of practical activities that you might do with your child.

Look, cover, write, check

Look, cover, write, check is a strategy taught in schools which can also be used at home. Write the words your child is learning in the first column of a three- or four-column table. Ask your child to look at the spelling and read the word out loud, then to cover it, write the spelling in the next column then uncover the original spelling to check if they have got it right. The additional blank columns can be used for corrections or extra practice.

Flash cards

Create a double set of the words your child finds tricky to spell. They pick up two cards at a time until they find a pair. Ask them to spell the word out to you verbally.

Word searches and crossword puzzles

There are internet sites for both these activities as well as many printed books and magazines.

Tic Tac Toe

Create a 'noughts and crosses' grid and provide your child and another player with a face-down pile of the words they are learning and a different colour marker for each player. Players take it in turns to choose a spelling from the pile, read it, memorise the spelling, then write it in one of the grid spaces. The winner is the first to get three-in-a-row correctly spelt words.

Computer or tablet

Give your child the opportunity to type the words they are learning and to experiment with text fonts, sizes and colours.

Creating a good learning environment

As children learn best when they do not feel under pressure, distracted or tired, it is important that your child is:

- positive
- comfortable about making mistakes
- not rushed
- in a quiet, calm working place
- encouraged to check their work.

The importance of reading

Finally, encourage your child to read, read, read! Not only does reading improve their spelling and vocabulary, it stimulates their imagination and is a relaxing pastime in the midst of busy lives too often dominated by screens. Remember, the impact of you reading *to* and *with* your child should never be underestimated. It fosters a love of reading for pleasure – not just for the skill – and is an opportunity for you and your child to bond.

Starter test

1. **Add a letter or letters to the digraph 'ow' to make five words. You can add letters before, after or both. Write your words on the lines below. One has been done for you.**

   bowl ....

   ....

   5 marks

2. **Write what you see in the pictures below. Write the number of the things you see in words.**

   a) I can see ....

   b) I can see ....

   4 marks

3. Unscramble the letters to make words with a split digraph. Use the pictures to help you.

a) l a m e f ....

b) e d b r i ....

c) a t e p l ....

d) s l d e i ....

4 marks

4. Add the endings -ing, -ed and -er to each verb below.

a) walk ....

b) hunt ....

c) buzz ....

d) jump ....

12 marks

5. **Match each word on the left with a word in the box to make a compound word. Write the compound word on the line.**

ground	step	ring	dog

a) foot ....

b) hot ....

c) fair ....

d) ear ....

4 marks

6. **Unscramble these words which all start with the prefix un- and write the correct spellings on the lines.**

a) r c l e a u n ....

b) t y i d u n ....

c) h a p y p u n ....

d) k d i n u n ....

4 marks

7. **Write the missing days of the week.**

.... Tuesday .... Thursday

.... Saturday ....

4 marks

8. Add the endings -er and -est to each word in bold to compare two or more people or things.

a) Jack ran **fast**, Karl ran .... but Cecile ran the ....

b) This building is **tall**, that one is .... but the one over there is the ....

c) Petra has a **loud** voice, Floyd's is even .... but Keir's is the ....

6 marks

9. Use the pictures to help you write the answers.

a) I have the trigraph 'air' and I rhyme with **pair**.

....

b) I have the trigraph 'ear' and I rhyme with **bear**.

....

c) I have the trigraph 'igh' and I rhyme with **right**.

....

d) I have the trigraph 'tch' and I rhyme with **pitch**.

....

e) I have the split digraph a–e and I rhyme with **take**.

....

f) I have the digraph 'ow' and I rhyme with **now**.

....

6 marks

10. Tick the words that Zac has spelt correctly. Write the corrections on the lines below.

Spelling words	✓
bank	
giv	
wach	
hav	
rich	
lov	
pinck	
mutch	

....

....

....

6 marks

Total: ______ / 55 marks

The j sound

Teaching note

The **j** sound can be spelt in many different ways:

- When it comes before 'a', 'o' and 'u', it is always spelt 'j'.
- When the **j** sound follows a short vowel sound, it is spelt 'dge' – for example, fudge.
- When the sound follows a long vowel sound, it is spelt 'ge' – for example, page.
- When it comes before 'e', 'i' and 'y', it is often spelt 'g' – for example, gem.

Challenge 1

1 Say each word out loud. Decide if it has a short vowel sound like 'fudge' or a long vowel sound like 'huge'. Write the words in the correct column in the table below.
Remember that 'a', 'e', 'i', 'o' and 'u' are the vowels.

dodge	**huge**	**page**	**ledge**	**badge**
smudge	**rage**	**stage**	**fudge**	**cage**

Short vowel sound	Long vowel sound

10 marks

Challenge 2

1 Use the clues to help you fill in the missing letters.

a) Can be found between two gardens and needs to be cut when it grows too tall.

h	e			

b) You might spread this on your toast.

		m

c) Tells you the number of years you have lived.

a		

d) Another word for very big.

		a	n	t

4 marks

Challenge 3

1 Find the word with a **j** sound in each sentence which has been spelt incorrectly. Write the correct spelling on the line.

a) Sami had lots of enerdgey after his nap. ....

b) I asked Dad to open the gar of honey. ....

c) Our teacher told us to chanje for P.E. ....

d) A jiraffe has a really long neck. ....

4 marks

Total: ______ / 18 marks

Had a go ☐ Getting there ☐ Got it! ☐

The s sound spelt 'c' before 'e', 'i' and 'y'

Teaching note

The **s** sound can be spelt 'c' when it comes before 'e', 'i' and 'y'.

Challenge 1

1 Write the words in the correct column in the table below.

race icy city cell fancy dancer
cinema fierce cigar cycle slice lacy

s sound spelt 'c' before 'e'	s sound spelt 'c' before 'i'	s sound spelt 'c' before 'y'

12 marks

Challenge 2

1 Fill in the missing letters in these words that have an **s** sound spelt 'c'.

a) Somewhere you go to watch films. .... m a

b) The amount you pay for something. p r ....

c) A place you go to watch acrobats and clowns. .... u s

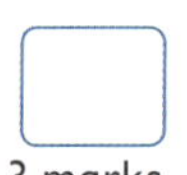

3 marks

Challenge 3

1 Use the clues to complete the crossword.

Across

4. What you do when you ride a bike
6. A round 2D shape
8. Someone who dances
10. The plural of mouse
11. A word used to describe something that is freezing cold

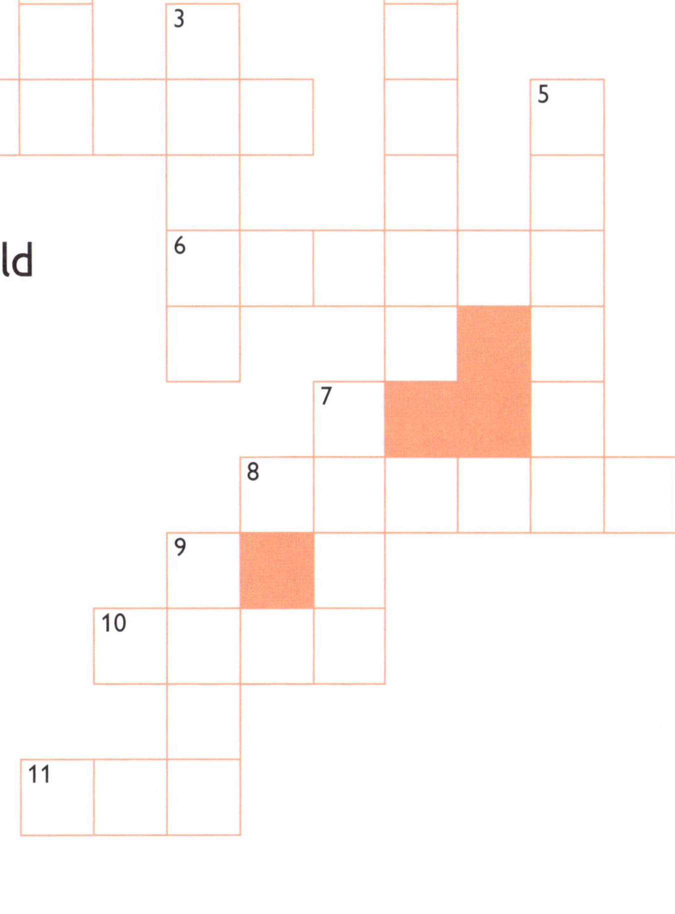

Down

1. A word you might use to describe curry
2. A word used to describe a rubber ball
3. A piece of something such as bread or cake
5. An angry or aggressive animal or person
7. A running contest
9. A large town

11 marks

Total: ______ / 26 marks

 Had a go ☐  Getting there ☐  Got it! ☐

Silent letters

Teaching note

When the letters 'g' or 'k' come before the letter 'n', we do not say them. We call them **silent letters**.

Challenge 1

1 Write the four words from the box that have silent letters on the lines below.

kitchen	**know**	**skip**	**knight**
gnaw	**garden**	**knot**	

....

....

4 marks

Challenge 2

1 Write the missing silent letters at the start of each word.

a) .... n o c k

b) .... n u c k l e

c) .... n a s h

d) .... n o b

4 marks

2 Now write each word on the lines below.

....

....

4 marks

Challenge 3

1 Find the word in each sentence that is missing its silent letter. Write the correct spelling on the line.

a) Edith nelt down to stroke the dog.

....

b) Monty spent ages nawing on the bone.

....

c) Anya used a sharp nife to cut the steak.

....

d) Our friends have five nomes in their garden.

....

e) Edna is nitting a woolly scarf for the winter.

....

f) Someone is nocking on the door.

....

6 marks

Total: ______ / 18 marks

Had a go ☐ Getting there ☐ Got it! ☐

The r sound spelt 'wr' at the beginning of words

Teaching note The spelling 'wr' at the beginning of words is said 'r'. The 'w' is a **silent letter**.

Challenge 1

1 Write the four words that have a silent 'w'.

wind	wrapper	wrong	wand
wreck	wrestle	whip	

....

....

4 marks

Challenge 2

1 Unscramble the letters to find words that start with a silent 'w'.

a) p a w r

....

b) t e w r o

....

c) g g w r i l e

....

d) o n w r g

....

4 marks

Challenge 3

1 Find the word in each sentence that starts with the **r** sound but has been spelt incorrectly. Write the word with the correct spelling on the line.

a) Rebecca rote her name at the end of her report.

....

b) Nuala carefully rapped Keir's present.

....

c) Ivor riggles in his bed when he's feeling restless.

....

d) Poppy likes restling with her rescue dog.

....

e) Claire has ritten a letter to her running buddy.

....

5 marks

Total: ______ / 13 marks

 Had a go 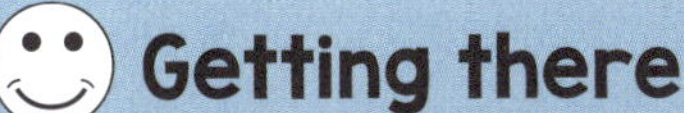  

Getting there

Got it!

The i sound spelt 'y' at the end of words

Teaching note When the **i** sound comes at the end of words, it is usually spelt 'y'.

Challenge 1

1. Read the words and find the ones that end in 'y' with an **i** sound. Write these words on the lines below.

....

3 marks

Challenge 2

1 Complete each sentence by adding a word that ends in 'y' with an **i** sound.

a) If you .... hard, you will soon know your spellings.

b) Bernie likes to .... her kite on the beach.

c) Dad is hanging the washing out to ....

d) Vincent began to .... when he hurt his knee.

4 marks

Challenge 3

1 Write a sentence in answer to each question. Remember that a sentence starts with a capital letter and ends with a full stop.

a) Where is the sun?

....

b) What is on the bear's nose?

....

4 marks

Total: ______ / 11 marks

Had a go ☐ Getting there ☐ Got it! ☐

Words ending in -tion

Teaching note

The sound **shun** which comes at the end of some English words can be spelt -tion.

Challenge 1

1. Read each word out loud, then cover, write and check. Use the second line to correct any mistakes or for extra practice.

fiction ....

station ....

motion ....

fraction ....

nation ....

5 marks

2. Write a sentence using one of the words above.

Remember that a sentence starts with a capital letter and ends with a full stop.

....

....

2 marks

Challenge 2

1 Use the words in Challenge 1 to answer the clues.

a) A place where you can catch a train. ....

b) Another word for movement. ....

c) The opposite of fact. ....

d) Another word for a country. ....

4 marks

Challenge 3

1 The words in the box have been spelt as they sound. Complete each sentence with the correct spelling.

menshun	fracshun	secshun

a) Orla said, "A .... is part of a whole."

b) The teacher read the first .... of the book.

c) Bruce did not .... that it was his birthday.

3 marks

Total: ______ / 14 marks

Had a go  Getting there  Got it!

Progress test 1

1. **Fill in the missing letters to make words where the s sound is spelt 'c'.**

   a) A white grain you might eat with curry

   r ....

   b) Six-sided shapes you roll in a game

   .... i ....

   c) Frozen water

   .... e

   d) Bigger than a town

   .... y

4 marks

2. **Find the words in the box that end in 'y' with an i sound. Write the words on the lines below.**

reply	key	sly	dry	stay	fry

....

....

4 marks

3. Find a word with a j sound in each sentence that has been spelt incorrectly. Write the correct spelling on the line.

a) Mum helped me put on my gacket. ....

b) Pietro likes to do majic tricks. ....

c) Erin is going to goin the drama club. ....

d) The jiant lives in a deep, dark cave. ....

4 marks

4. Complete the missing rhyming words in the verse below. The words all end in the i sound spelt 'y'.

In sunny J ....

My kite does .... l ....

High in the .... k ....

3 marks

5. Write the missing letters to complete the words ending in a shun sound.

a) Keira likes books which tell you facts, but Bev prefers ....

f		c				

b) "Meet me at the bus ....," said Marcus.

	t	a				

c) The wizard made a magic ....

p					

3 marks

6. Unscramble the letters of each word in bold to make a word with a silent letter. Write the word on the line.

a) Cerys **d e p w p a r** Ollie's present. ....

b) Mrs Todd said the sum was **g n r o w**. ....

c) Finn **e t w r o** a postcard to Karim. ....

d) Dad is **g i n w i t r** a letter. ....

4 marks

7. Use the pictures to help you complete these words which have a j sound.

a) p ....

b) h e ....

c) b r i ....

d) f r i ....

e) o r a n ....

f) c a ....

6 marks

8. Add the missing silent letters to complete each word.

a) The angry beast .... a s h e d his sharp teeth.

b) Mum hurt her .... u c k l e s when she banged on the door.

c) Our dog likes to .... a w on a bone.

d) Maya .... e e l s down to stroke the kitten.

4 marks

Total: ______ / 32 marks

The ul sound spelt 'le' at the end of words

Most words ending in an **ul** sound have the spelling 'le'.

Challenge 1

1 Write the **four** words that end with an **ul** sound on the lines below.

apple

table

school

smell

bottle

stable

....

....

4 marks

Challenge 2

1 Choose a word to complete each sentence below.

middle	eagle	little	bubbles

a) Ali sits in the .... of her two best friends.

b) Raj blows .... for his baby sister.

c) Molly has a .... brother called Jamie.

d) The .... spread its wings and flew away.

4 marks

Challenge 3

1 Use the clues to complete the crossword.

1 U

2 S

3 D

4 A

5 T

6 W

Across

4. Connects your leg to your foot.
5. Lives in the sea and has a thick, hard shell.
6. A movement a worm might make.

Down

1. Your mum's brother is your ....
2. A place where horses are kept.
3. Two of the same thing.

6 marks

Total: ______ / 14 marks

Had a go ☐ Getting there ☐ Got it! ☐

The ul sound spelt 'el' at the end of words

Teaching note

The spelling 'el' at the end of words often comes after the letters 'm', 'n', 'r', 's', 'v' and 'w' but it can also come after other letters.

Challenge 1

1. Read each word out loud, then cover, write and check. Use the second line to correct any mistakes or for extra practice.

towel ....

squirrel ....

camel ....

travel ....

tunnel ....

kennel ....

parcel ....

label ....

8 marks

Challenge 2

1. Use suitable words from Challenge 1 to complete the sentences below.

   a) Dad had to .... through a long ....

b) Our dog has a .... in his ....

c) Eva stuck the .... on the ....

6 marks

Challenge 3

1 Write a sentence about what you see in each picture.

Remember that a sentence starts with a capital letter and ends with a full stop.

I can see…

a) ....

....

b) ....

....

4 marks

Total: ______ / 18 marks

Had a go ☐ Getting there ☐ Got it! ☐

The ul sound spelt 'al' at the end of words

Teaching note

A **noun** is a naming word for a person, place, thing or animal. A **noun phrase** is a group of words that provides more information about the noun in the phrase.

Challenge 1

1 Write the correct **noun phrase** under the picture it describes.

animal hospital	special medal	local festival
magical coral	metal pedal	

....

....

....

....

....

5 marks

Challenge 2

1 Use the clues to help you fill in the missing letters.

a) The opposite of a lowercase letter.

c	a					

b) The amount you get when you add two or more numbers together.

t	o			

c) A word that can describe a king, queen, prince or princess.

r	o			

3 marks

Challenge 3

1 Choose two noun phrases from Challenge 1. Write a sentence containing each noun phrase.

Remember that a sentence starts with a capital letter and ends with a full stop.

a) ....

....

b) ....

....

4 marks

Total: ______ / 12 marks

Had a go ☐ Getting there ☐ Got it! ☐

The ul sound spelt 'il' at the end of words

When learning to spell words ending in 'il', split them into syllables and stress the 'il' sound. For example, ger-*bil*.

Challenge 1

1 Write the correct word under each picture.

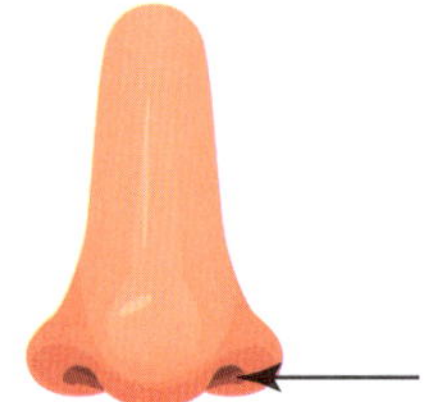

a) g e r ....

b) n .... s t ....

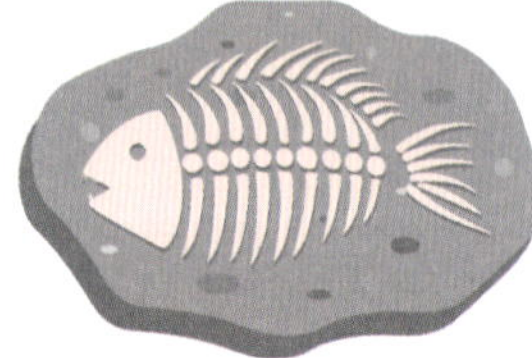

c) p .... n c ....

d) f .... s s ....

4 marks

2 Write a sentence containing one of the words above.

Remember that a sentence starts with a capital letter and ends with a full stop.

....

....

2 marks

Challenge 2

1 Pedro is struggling with his sentences. Help him by writing the correct word on the line.

a) It's one hour .... bedtime.

Is it until or untill?

b) The month after March is ....

Is it Aprul or April?

c) The .... monster chased the fairies around the forest.

Is it evil or eval?

3 marks

Challenge 3

1 Unscramble the letters to find the words ending in 'il'

a) b g e r i l ....

b) i l s f o s ....

c) i l d a f f d o ....

d) u p p i l ....

4 marks

Total: ______ / 13 marks

Had a go ☐ Getting there ☐ Got it! ☐

The or sound spelt 'a' before 'l' and 'll'

Tip The **or** sound is often spelt 'a' before 'l' and 'll'.

Challenge 1

1 Read each word out loud, then cover, write and check. Use the second line to correct any mistakes or for extra practice.

ball ....

all ....

also ....

always ....

bald ....

walk ....

6 marks

Challenge 2

1 Complete each sentence with the correct spelling of the missing word.

stalk **stallk** **stal** **stall**

a) The flower's .... bends over in the breeze.

b) We buy fruit from a market ....

2 marks

Challenge 3

1 Find two words in each sentence that have an **or** sound and that have been spelt incorrectly. Write the correct spellings in the correct column of the table below.

a) Grace's brother, who is caled Sonny, is quite tal.

b) We allways tallk to our grandparents at the weekend.

c) The wallker had allmost reached the top of the hill.

d) Tom has left his bal in the halway.

Words with 'al'	Words with 'all'
....	....
....	....
....	....
....	....

8 marks

Total: ______ / 16 marks

 Getting there  Got it! 

Words with an 'o' and words with an 'ey' spelling

The letter 'o' can make more than one sound. Sometimes, it makes a long **oh** sound and sometimes it makes a short **uh** sound.

Challenge 1

1 Say these words out loud then write them in the correct column in the table.

other cover over stone brother

mole bone mother

Short vowel sound uh spelt 'o'	Long vowel sound oh spelt 'o'
....	....
....	....
....	....
....	....

8 marks

Challenge 2

To make the plural of most words that end with an **ee** sound spelt 'ey', just add 's'.

1 Say these words out loud. Write the ones with an **ee** sound spelt 'ey' on the lines.

key obey trolley money

they jockey grey

4 marks

Challenge 3

1 Use the words in the box to write two sentences about what is happening in the picture.

Remember that a sentence starts with a capital letter and ends with a full stop.

monkey	donkeys	turkeys	journey	valley

4 marks

Total: ____ / 16 marks

 Had a go  Getting there  Got it! 

Progress test 2

1. Add the ending 'al', 'il', 'el' or 'le' to complete each word.

a) fidd....................

b) trav....................

c) roy....................

d) fin....................

e) dribb....................

f) stenc....................

g) equ....................

h) tins....................

8 marks

2. Insert the missing letters to make words with an i sound spelt 'y'.

"I s ....

with my little eye

something beginning with 'f'."

".......... ...."

2 marks

3. Complete the sentences with the plural of the following words.

Remember that plural means more than one of something.

jockey	chimney	key

a) Mum hangs her .... on a hook.

b) The .... rode to the starting line.

c) Smoke billowed out of all the ....

3 marks

4. Write the correct spelling of the words in bold on the lines below.

a) The **jewal / jewel** sparkled in the sunlight.

b) Gran likes **caramel / caramal** sweets.

c) The **vowels / vowils** are a, e, i, o and u.

d) Christie painted his **model / modal** airplane.

....

....

4 marks

5. Unscramble the letters to find words ending in -tion.

a) t o i n i c f ....

b) t s a t i n o ....

c) i o n t o m ....

d) o t i n r a f c ....

e) t o i n a n ....

5 marks

6. The words in bold have an or sound but have been spelt incorrectly. Write the correct spellings on the lines below.

"Be careful you don't **fal** on the ice," Angus **caled**. "You're **wallking** and kicking the **bal** at the same time. It's unsafe."

"What are you **tallking** about? **Al** the ice has gone," replied Bea.

....

....

....

6 marks

7. Unscramble the letters to make words with a silent 'k' or a silent 'g'. Write the words on the lines.

a) o c k k n ....

b) o m e g n ....

c) i t k n ....

d) a w g n ....

4 marks

8. Insert the missing letters to make words with an s sound spelt 'c'.

a) n ....

b) r ....

c) s p ....

3 marks

9. Choose the correct spelling from each pair of words in bold and write it on the lines below.

a) Please **rite / write** the date in your book.

b) Hans knocked on the **wrong / rong** door.

c) Stan's puppy **wriggled / riggled** under the hedge.

d) Dad **rapped / wrapped** my scarf round my neck.

....

....

4 marks

Total: ______ / 39 marks

Adding -es to nouns and verbs ending in 'y'

Teaching note

If a noun or verb ends in 'y', change 'y' to 'i' before adding -es. For example, cry → cries.

Challenge 1

1 Add -es to make the plural of the following nouns.

a) lady ....

b) party ....

c) story ....

d) city ....

4 marks

Challenge 2

1 Write the correct form of the verbs in bold to complete the sentences.

a) Enya (**try**) .... hard at school.

b) Harry (**spy**) .... his brother in the park.

c) Jing (**copy**) .... down the homework task.

3 marks

Challenge 3

1 Underline the **noun** in each noun phrase below.

Remember that a noun is a naming word for a person, place, animal or thing.

a) the annoying fly

b) the kind aunty

c) the big city

d) the pretty fairy

e) the crying baby

f) the ripe berry

6 marks

2 Write the **plural** of each noun phrase from Question 1 on the lines below.

a) ....

b) ....

c) ....

d) ....

e) ....

f) ....

6 marks

Total: ______ / 19 marks

Had a go ☐ Getting there ☐ Got it! ☐

Adding -ed, -ing and -y

Teaching note

A **root word** is the basic form of a word where no **prefixes** or **suffixes** have been added. If a root word ends in 'y' and there is a **consonant** before it, change the 'y' to 'i' before adding the suffix -ed. For example, copy → copied.

Challenge 1

1 Add the suffix -ed to each verb below, following the spelling rule where it applies.

a) wait ....
b) cry ....

c) hurry ....
d) jump ....

e) study ....
f) spy ....

g) reply ....
h) walk ....

i) call ....
j) apply ....

10 marks

Teaching note

The letter 'y' stays when adding the suffix -ing. For example, copy → copying.

Challenge 2

1 Add the correct suffix to the words in the box to complete the sentences below.

worry	**marry**	**copy**	**carry**

a) Flo is getting .... next week.

b) Our teacher is .... the maths papers.

c) The bees are .... pollen from flower to flower.

d) Gran was .... about the baby crying.

4 marks

Teaching note

The letter 'e' at the end of a root word is dropped before adding the letter 'y'. For example, bone → bony.

Challenge 3

1 Write the correct form of the words in bold to complete the sentences.

a) Otto has **wave** .... hair.

b) Fabian is very **nose** ....

c) Yasmin has a **shine** .... new bike.

d) The twins like **noise** .... music!

4 marks

Total: ______ / 18 marks

Had a go ☐ Getting there ☐ Got it! ☐

Adding -er and -est

Teaching note

If a root word ends in 'e' with a consonant before it, the 'e' is dropped before adding the suffixes -er and -est. For example, close → closer, closest. For words that end in 'y', change the 'y' to 'I' before adding -er and -est

Challenge 1

1 Solve the clues then write the missing words.

a) Someone who likes to **hike**.

b) Someone who tells **jokes**.

c) Someone who likes to **dance**.

d) Someone whose job is to **write**.

4 marks

Teaching note

Sometimes, we want to compare two or more things in a sentence. For example, 'Yesterday was **cold**, today is **colder** but tomorrow will be the **coldest**'.

Challenge 2

1. Add the suffixes to each word on the left.

Words	Add -er	Add -est
nice	....	....
late	....	....
safe	....	....
large	....	....

8 marks

Challenge 3

1. Follow the spelling rule to complete the following sentences with the correct form of the adjectives in bold.

a) Lucia is **lazy**, Pol is .... but Priti is the ....

b) Rajiv is **heavy**, Cal is .... but Drew is the ....

c) Sydney's room is **tidy**, Mo's is .... but Tilly's is the ....

6 marks

Total: ______ / 18 marks

Had a go ☐  Getting there ☐ Got it! ☐

Doubling final consonants

Teaching note

When adding -ed, -ing, -er, -est and -y to words of one syllable that end in a single consonant after a single vowel, the last consonant is doubled. For example, pat → patted, patting, patter. This keeps the short vowel sound short.

Challenge 1

1 Use the spelling rule to add the suffixes -ed and -ing to the words in the box.

bat	**float**	**walk**	**stop**	**whip**
	calm	**click**	**hop**	

Add -ed and -ing and double the final consonant to keep a short vowel sound		**Add -ed and -ing where the final consonant is not doubled**	
-ed	-ing	-ed	-ing
....	....	....	....
....	....	....	....
....	....	....	....
....	....	....	....

16 marks

Challenge 2

1 Complete each comparative sentence with the correct form of the words in the box.

sun	**fun**

a) Yesterday was ...., today is .... but tomorrow is going to be the ....

b) Tigan's jokes are ...., Lin's are .... but Eric's are the ....

6 marks

Challenge 3

1 Find the words that have been spelt incorrectly in the text. Use the information to complete the sentences below using the correct spelling.

Fabien is a great drumer. He wears a bagy jumper and likes huming and taping his feet as he drums. It's a suny day, so he has taken his drum kit outside. His pupy, called Misha, watches him play, often runing up and down the garden.

a) It's a .... day.

b) Fabien is a great ....

c) He wears a .... jumper.

d) Misha the .... is .... in the garden.

e) Fabien likes .... and .... his feet.

7 marks

Total: ______ / 29 marks

Had a go ☐ Getting there ☐ Got it! ☐

The suffixes -ment, -ness, -ful, -less and -ly

Tip If a suffix starts with a consonant, you don't usually have to change the spelling of the word you are adding it to.

Challenge 1

1 Change these verbs into nouns by adding the suffix -ment.

enjoy	pay	agree	excite	treat	achieve

....

....

....

6 marks

Tip If a word ends in 'y' with a consonant before it and has more than one syllable, the 'y' is changed to 'i' before a suffix is added.

Challenge 2

1 Add the suffix -ment, -ness or -ful to each of the following words.

happy	play	merry	pave	care

....

....

....

5 marks

Teaching note An **adverb** tells you more about the verb in a sentence. Many adverbs end in the suffix -ly.

Challenge 3

1 Add the suffix -less or -ly to the words in the box. Write the words in the correct column in the table below.

tidy	**calm**	**hope**
use	**quiet**	**penny**
happy	**sad**	**funny**
care	**harm**	**life**

-less	-ly
....	....
....	....
....	....
....	....
....	....
....	....

12 marks

Total: ______ / 23 marks

 Had a go ☐  Getting there ☐  Got it! ☐

The zh sound spelt 's'

Teaching note In some words, the letter 's' is pronounced **zh**. For example, vision.

Challenge 1

1 Say each word in the box out loud. Listen to the sound made by the letter 's'. Write the words in the correct column in the table.

division **revision** **crispy** **tinsel** **usual** **rest**

's' pronounced zh	's' pronounced s
....	....
....	....
....	....

6 marks

Challenge 2

1 Listen to the sound the 's' makes when you say the words 'television' and 'treasure' out loud. Write a sentence containing each word to answer the questions.

a) Where might you find a **television**?

....

....

b) Where might you find **treasure**?

....

....

4 marks

Challenge 3

1 Add the suffix -ed, -s or -ing to the verb 'measure' to complete each sentence.

a) I watch as Dad .... the piece of wood.

b) Gregor is .... the piece of wood.

c) Yesterday, Sandrine .... how tall her sister is.

3 marks

Total: ______ / 13 marks

Had a go ☐ Getting there ☐ Got it! ☐

Progress test 3

1. Write the correct ul ending to complete the words in the sentences.

el	al	le

a) William was a l o y .... servant to the king.

b) Luke has moved to the next l e v .... in reading.

c) Farmer Joe led the horse into the s t a b ....

d) London is the c a p i t .... city of England.

e) Oscar made a paper a n g .... for the Christmas tree.

5 marks

2. Write the plural of each word.

a) ferry ....

b) lily ....

c) jelly ....

d) cherry ....

4 marks

3. Complete each sentence with the correct spelling of the verbs in the box.

wrap	hop	clap	pat	hum	drop

a) The children are .... for the players.

b) Vincent is .... the dog.

c) Kave is .... Iona's present.

d) Faith keeps .... her pencil.

e) The kangaroo is .... across the field.

f) Yolande and Xavier are .... a tune.

6 marks

4. Unscramble the letters to make words with a silent 'k'.

a) t i t i n g n k ....

b) n k c u k l e ....

c) o c k k n ....

d) k e e n ....

4 marks

5. Add the correct suffix to the adjectives in bold to complete each sentence.

a) This little piggy is **fat**, that little piggy is even .... but the little piggy over there is the .... of all.

b) The film made Sophie and Cal feel **sad**, but Gwyn felt even .... However, Dejay felt the .... of them all.

c) Daddy Bear's boiled egg was **runny**, Mummy Bear's was even .... but Baby Bear's was the ....

6 marks

6. Write the words with a silent 'w' on the lines below.

wriggle	waddle	wink	wrapper
wonder	warp	writing	

....

3 marks

7. Write the missing letters in the words with the s sound spelt 'c' to complete the sentences.

a) Freddie works in the .... i .... of Manchester.

b) Isaac got the prize for the best f .... dress.

c) Ronil made a funny f ....

d) The prisoner escaped from his .... l l.

4 marks

8. Add an appropriate suffix to each word in bold. Write the word on the line.

a) Rae was full of **excite** .... when she heard about the party.

b) Jude's new puppy is very **play** ....

c) Gran is **care** .... when she crosses the road.

3 marks

Total: ______ / 35 marks

The er sound spelt 'or' and the or sound spelt 'ar' after 'w'

Challenge 1

1 Write the words in the box in the correct place in the table.

word	war	towards	work
worm	warm	worse	warn

'or' spelling pronounced er after 'w'	'ar' spelling pronounced or after 'w'
....	....
....	....
....	....
....	....

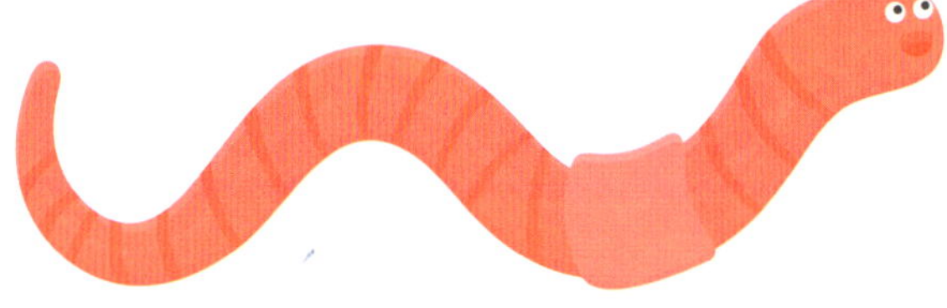

8 marks

Challenge 2

1 Add a suffix to the words in the box to complete the sentences below.

work	warn	warm

a) Maya is .... on her times tables.

b) There was a .... about bad weather on the radio.

c) Mum .... up some soup for me.

3 marks

Challenge 3

1 Unscramble the letters to make words with an **or** sound spelt 'ar'. Write the words on the lines.

a) Jan is visiting her gran in the hospital **r a d w**.

....

b) Bill is painting the **d w a r r o e b**. ....

c) Thomas's great-grandad told us about his time in the **r a w**.

....

d) "I think Sneezy is the funniest **w d f r a**," said Dad.

....

4 marks

Total: ______ / 15 marks

Had a go ☐ Getting there ☐ Got it! ☐

Compound words

Teaching note

A **compound word** is made by joining two words to make one word. For example, play + ground = playground.

Challenge 1

1 Use the pictures to write six compound words.

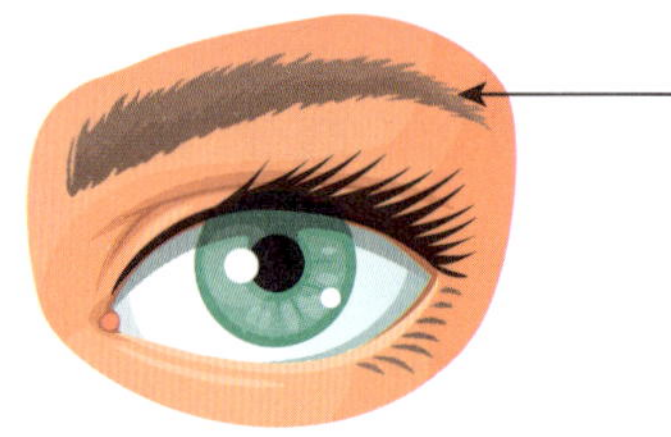

....

....

....

6 marks

Challenge 2

1 Write a word that can be added to each word to form a compound word.

a) ward .... **b)** toe ....

c) car .... **d)** hand ....

4 marks

Challenge 3

1. The compound words in the sentences below have been jumbled up. Work out the correct words and write them on the lines.

   a) Jenni put her teasill on the windowcup.

   ....

   b) Filo likes toast with strawfast jam for breakberry.

   ....

   c) Dad put his newsshelf on the bookpaper.

   ....

   d) A bumblebush buzzed around the rosebee.

   ....

   ☐ 8 marks

Total: ______ / 18 marks

Had a go ☐  Getting there ☐  Got it! ☐

Contractions

Teaching tip

A **contraction** is created when two words are combined and some letters are omitted. The missing letters are indicated by an apostrophe. For example, I am → I'm, where the apostrophe indicates the missing letter 'a' from 'am'.

Challenge 1

1 Write the contractions in full by inserting the missing letters indicated by the apostrophes. One has been done for you.

I'll *I will*

a) mustn't ....

b) didn't ....

c) shouldn't ....

d) hasn't ....

e) couldn't ....

f) haven't ....

6 marks

Challenge 2

1 Insert an apostrophe in each word in bold to indicate where a letter is missing.

a) We **a r e n t** going swimming today.

b) **T h e y r e** moving house next month.

c) **S h e s** buying a new bike.

d) Look, **t h e r e s** Mark with his mum.

4 marks

Challenge 3

1 Write the contracted form of the words on the left.

a) we are →

b) he is →

c) he had →

d) I will →

4 marks

Total: ______ / 14 marks

Had a go ☐ Getting there  Got it! ☐

Apostrophes to show belonging

An **apostrophe** can be used to show that something belongs to someone or something. For example, Harry's hat – the hat belonging to Harry.

Challenge 1

1 Write each phrase on the left as a noun phrase with an apostrophe to show possession. One has been done for you.

the tail belonging to the dog

the dog's tail

a) the gloves belonging to the lady

....

b) the bike belonging to Nadia

....

c) the car belonging to Mum

....

3 marks

Challenge 2

1 Underline the words in the sentences below that should have an apostrophe. Write the word on the line and add the apostrophe in the correct place.

a) The cat is sleeping in the dogs bed. ....

b) There is a birds nest at the top of the tree.

....

c) Mum stood on Dads toe. ....

d) Joes shoes are muddy. ....

4 marks

Challenge 3

1 Write the words in bold in the correct column in the table below.

Jaz's sums were wrong.

Jaz **isn't** sure how to add the numbers.

Freddie's hurt his foot.

The dog's paw is sore.

Apostrophe to show a contraction	Apostrophe to show possession
....	....
....	....

4 marks

Total: ______ / 11 marks

Homophones and near-homophones

Teaching note

A **homophone** is a word that sounds the same as another word but has a different spelling and meaning. For example, here / hear.

Challenge 1

1. Select the correct homophone from the box to complete the sentences below.

too two	**sea see**	**blue blew**

a) We're going to the zoo and you can come

....

b) Bethan has .... tickets for the zoo.

c) We cheered loudly when we saw the sparkling blue

....

d) Can you .... Mum's missing ring?

e) The wind .... all night long.

f) The sky is .... today.

6 marks

Tip

A **near-homophone** is a word that sounds *almost* the same as another word but has a different spelling and meaning. For example, quite / quiet.

Challenge 2

1 Write the correct near-homophone to complete each sentence.

peace **peas**

a) Miles doesn't like .... with his dinner.

quiet **quite**

b) It's very .... in our classroom.

won **one**

c) Sian easily .... the running race.

3 marks

Challenge 3

1 Write the correct spelling of the five homophones in the sentence below.

Clever Chloe new their wood bee an answer too the problem.

....

....

....

5 marks

Total: ______ / 14 marks

Had a go ☐ Getting there ☐ Got it! ☐

Tricky words

Tip Some words are tricky to spell because they don't follow the spelling or phoneme rules you have learned.

Challenge 1

1. Read each word out loud, then cover, write and check. Use the second line to correct any mistakes or for extra practice.

door ....

wild ....

children ....

climb ....

only ....

pretty ....

sugar ....

eye ....

any ....

9 marks

Challenge 2

1 The word 'calm' has an 'al' digraph which is pronounced **ar**. Write two more words that have the same spelling pattern. Use the images to help you.

....

2 marks

2 The word 'great' has an 'ea' digraph which is pronounced as a long **a**. Write two more words that have the same spelling which makes this sound. Use the images to help you.

....

2 marks

Tip A **mnemonic** is a memory tool that can help you remember how to spell tricky words. For example, the word 'said' could be remembered as **S**ally **a**nd **I** **d**ance.

Challenge 3

1 Make up your own mnemonic for the word 'water'.

....

1 mark

Total: ______ / 14 marks

Had a go ☐ Getting there ☐ Got it! ☐

Progress test 4

1. Add a suffix to the words in the box to complete each sentence below.

reply	fly	cry	copy

a) The planes are .... across the blue sky.

b) Gigi .... my spellings this morning.

c) Bertie has .... to my letter.

d) My brother started .... when he hurt his toe.

4 marks

2. Write the plural of each noun phrase below.

a) the strong body ....

b) the little pony ....

c) the marching army ....

d) the red cherry ....

4 marks

3. Write the missing letters in the words with an or sound in the sentences below.

a) The old witch had a w .... on her chin.

b) The bath water was nice and w ....

c) Rex ran from the s .... of bees.

3 marks

4. Write the missing letters to complete each of the following words which have an ending that sounds like 'ul'.

a) The p e t .... was pretty, soft and delicate.

b) Hayley used a p e n c .... to write her name.

c) The p l u r .... of goose is geese.

d) Matt drove the car into the dark t u n n ....

4 marks

5. Complete the sentences with the correct spelling of the word from the boxes.

wont	won't	wo'nt

a) "Why .... you come to the park?"

the'res	**ther'es**	**there's**

b) Dad says .... a fair coming to town.

can't	**cann't**	**cant**

c) My baby brother .... speak yet.

shouldv'e	**should've**	**shoul'dve**

d) I .... learned my spellings better.

she'd	**shed**	**sh'ed**

e) Mum said .... take me shopping later.

5 marks

6. Add a suffix to the words in the box to complete each sentence below.

work	**warn**	**warm**

a) Dad has .... us about going too close to the fire.

b) It should be .... tomorrow.

c) Mrs Lee is .... in our school.

3 marks

7. **Change these adjectives into adverbs by adding the suffix -ly.**

a) tidy → ....

b) messy → ....

c) crazy → ....

3 marks

8. **Write the correct homophone to complete each sentence.**

knight / night **flower / flour** **hair / hare**

a) I saw an owl flying past our house last ....

b) Dad used .... to bake a cake.

c) A .... can run very fast.

3 marks

Total: ______ / 29 marks

Answers

Pages 6–11

1. Answers will vary. Examples: cow, how, low, mow, now, row, sow, tow, vow, wow, blow, crow, flow, show, slow, glow, own, owl **[5]**
2. **a)** two boxes **b)** three dresses **[4]**
3. **a)** flame **b)** bride **c)** plate **d)** slide **[4]**
4. **a)** walking, walked, walker
   b) hunting, hunted, hunter
   c) buzzing, buzzed, buzzer
   d) jumping, jumped, jumper **[12]**
5. **a)** footstep **b)** hotdog
   c) fairground **d)** earring **[4]**
6. **a)** unclear **b)** untidy
   c) unhappy **d)** unkind **[4]**
7. Monday, Wednesday, Friday, Sunday **[4]**
8. **a)** faster, fastest **b)** taller, tallest
   c) louder, loudest **[6]**
9. **a)** chair **b)** pear **c)** night
   d) witch **e)** bake **f)** cow **[6]**
10. give, watch, have, love, pink, much **[6]**

Pages 12–13

Challenge 1

1.

Short vowel sound	Long vowel sound
dodge	huge
ledge	page
badge	rage
smudge	stage
fudge	cage

[10]

Challenge 2

1. **a)** hedge **b)** jam **c)** age **d)** giant **[4]**

Challenge 3

1. **a)** energy **b)** jar **c)** change **d)** giraffe **[4]**

Pages 14–15

Challenge 1

1.

s sound spelt 'c' before 'e'	s sound spelt 'c' before 'i'	s sound spelt 'c' before 'y'
race cell dancer fierce slice	city cinema cigar	icy fancy cycle lacy

[12]

Challenge 2

1. **a)** cinema **b)** price **c)** circus **[3]**

Challenge 3

[11]

Pages 16–17

Challenge 1

1. know, knight, gnaw, knot **[4]**

Challenge 2

1. **a)** knock **b)** knuckle
   c) gnash **d)** knob **[4]**
2. Words copied correctly. **[4]**

Challenge 3

a) knelt **b)** gnawing **c)** knife
d) gnomes **e)** knitting **f)** knocking **[6]**

Pages 18–19

Challenge 1

1. wrapper, wrong, wreck, wrestle **[4]**

Challenge 2

1. **a)** wrap **b)** wrote **c)** wriggle **d)** wrong **[4]**

Challenge 3

1. **a)** Rebecca **wrote** her name at the end of her report.
   b) Nuala carefully **wrapped** Keir's present.
   c) Ivor **wriggles** in his bed when he's feeling restless.
   d) Poppy likes **wrestling** with her rescue dog.
   e) Claire has **written** a letter to her running buddy. **[5]**

Pages 20–21

Challenge 1

1. July, reply, cry **[3]**

Challenge 2

1. **a)** try **b)** fly **c)** dry **d)** cry **[4]**

Challenge 3

1. Answers may vary. Examples:
   a) The sun is in the sky.
   b) A fly is on the bear's nose. **[4]**

Pages 22–23

Challenge 1

1. Words spelt correctly. **[5]**
2. Answers will vary. **[2]**

Challenge 2

1. **a)** station **b)** motion **c)** fiction **d)** nation **[4]**

Challenge 3

1. **a)** fraction **b)** section **c)** mention **[3]**

Pages 24–27

1. **a)** rice **b)** dice **c)** ice **d)** city **[4]**
2. reply, sly, dry, fry **[4]**
3. **a)** jacket **b)** magic **c)** join **d)** giant **[4]**
4. In sunny **July** My kite does **fly**
   High in the **sky**. **[3]**
5. **a)** fiction **b)** station **c)** potion **[3]**
6. **a)** wrapped **b)** wrong **c)** wrote **d)** writing **[4]**
7. **a)** page **b)** hedge **c)** bridge
   d) fridge **e)** orange **f)** cage **[6]**
8. **a)** gnashed **b)** knuckles
   c) gnaw **d)** kneels **[4]**

Pages 28–29

Challenge 1

1. apple, table, bottle, stable **[4]**

Challenge 2

1. **a)** middle **b)** bubbles **c)** little **d)** eagle **[4]**

Challenge 3

1.

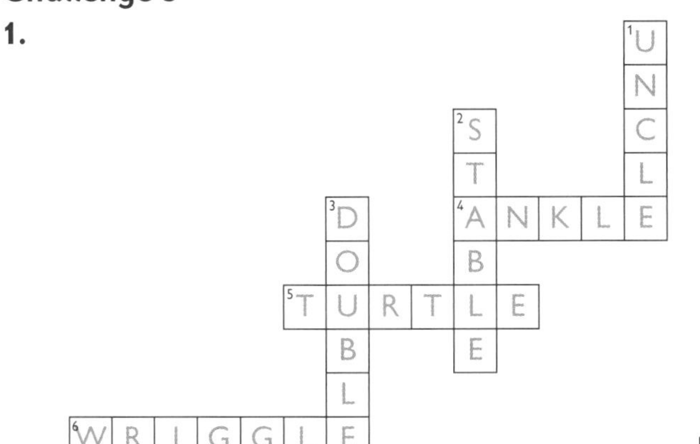

[6]

Pages 30–31

Challenge 1

1. Words spelt correctly. **[8]**

Challenge 2

1. **a)** travel, tunnel **b)** towel, kennel
   c) label, parcel **[6]**

Challenge 3

1. Answers will vary. Examples:
   a) I can see a squirrel eating a nut.
   b) I can see a camel walking on the sand. **[4]**

Pages 32–33

Challenge 1

1. Noun phrases spelt correctly under relevant picture. **[5]**

Challenge 2

1. **a)** capital **b)** total **c)** royal **[3]**

Challenge 3

1. Answers will vary. **[4]**

Pages 34–35

Challenge 1

1. **a)** gerbil **b)** nostril **c)** pencil **d)** fossil **[4]**
2. Answers will vary. **[2]**

Challenge 2

1. **a)** until **b)** April **c)** evil **[3]**

Challenge 3

1. **a)** gerbil **b)** fossil **c)** daffodil **d)** pupil **[4]**

Pages 36–37

Challenge 1

1. Words spelt correctly. **[6]**

Challenge 2

1. **a)** stalk **b)** stall **[2]**

Challenge 3

1.

Words with 'al'		Words with 'all'	
always	talk	called	tall
walker	almost	ball	hallway

[8]

Pages 38–39

Challenge 1

1.

Short vowel sound uh spelt 'o'		Long vowel sound uh spelt 'o'	
other	cover	over	stone
brother	mother	mole	bone

[8]

Challenge 2

1. key, trolley, money, jockey **[4]**

Challenge 3

1. Answers will vary. **[4]**

Pages 40–43

1. **a)** fiddle **b)** travel **c)** royal **d)** final
   e) dribble **f)** stencil **g)** equal **h)** tinsel **[8]**
2. spy, fly **[2]**
3. **a)** keys **b)** jockeys **c)** chimneys **[3]**

4. **a)** jewel **b)** caramel **c)** vowels **d)** model **[4]**
5. **a)** fiction **b)** station **c)** motion
   d) fraction **e)** nation **[5]**
6. fall, called, walking, ball, talking, All **[6]**
7. **a)** knock **b)** gnome **c)** knit **d)** gnaw **[4]**
8. **a)** nice **b)** rice/race **c)** spice/space **[3]**
9. **a)** write **b)** wrong
   c) wriggled **d)** wrapped **[4]**

Pages 44–45

Challenge 1

1. **a)** ladies **b)** parties **c)** stories **d)** cities **[4]**

Challenge 2

1. **a)** tries **b)** spies **c)** copies **[3]**

Challenge 3

1. **a)** fly **b)** aunty **c)** city
   d) fairy **e)** baby **f)** berry **[6]**
2. **a)** the annoying flies **b)** the kind aunties
   c) the big cities **d)** the pretty fairies
   e) the crying babies **f)** the ripe berries **[6]**

Pages 46–47

Challenge 1

1. **a)** waited **b)** cried **c)** hurried **d)** jumped
   e) studied **f)** spied **g)** replied **h)** walked
   i) called **j)** applied **[10]**

Challenge 2

1. **a)** married **b)** copying (accept carrying)
   c) carrying **d)** worried/worrying **[4]**

Challenge 3

1. **a)** wavy **b)** nosy **c)** shiny **d)** noisy **[4]**

Pages 48–49

Challenge 1

1. **a)** hiker **b)** joker **c)** dancer **d)** writer **[4]**

Challenge 2

1.

Words	Add -er	Add -est
nice	nicer	nicest
late	later	latest
safe	safer	safest
large	larger	largest

[8]

Challenge 3

1. **a)** lazier, laziest **b)** heavier, heaviest
   c) tidier, tidiest **[6]**

Pages 50–51

Challenge 1

1.

Add -ed and -ing and double the final consonant to keep a short vowel sound		Add -ed and -ing where the final consonant is not doubled	
-ed	-ing	-ed	-ing
batted	batting	floated	floating
stopped	stopping	walked	walking
whipped	whipping	calmed	calming
hopped	hopping	clicked	clicking

[16]

Challenge 2

1. **a)** sunny, sunnier, sunniest
   b) funny, funnier, funniest **[6]**

Challenge 3

1. **a)** It's a **sunny** day.
   b) Fabien is a **drummer**.
   c) He wears a **baggy** jumper.
   d) Misha the **puppy** is **running** in the garden.
   e) Fabien likes **humming** and **tapping** his feet. **[7]**

Pages 52–53

Challenge 1

1. enjoyment, payment, agreement, excitement, treatment, achievement **[6]**

Challenge 2

1. happiness, playful, merriment/merriness, pavement, careful **[5]**

Challenge 3

1.

-less		-ly	
hopeless	useless	tidily	calmly
penniless	careless	quietly	happily
harmless	lifeless	sadly	funnily

[12]

Pages 54–55

Challenge 1

1.

's' pronounced zh		's' pronounced s	
division	revision	crispy	tinsel
usual		rest	

[6]

Challenge 2

1. Answers will vary. Examples:
   a) You might find a television in the lounge.
   b) You might find treasure in a chest. **[4]**

Challenge 3

1. **a)** measures **b)** measuring **c)** measured **[3]**

Pages 56–59

1. **a)** loy**al** **b)** level **c)** stable
   d) capit**al** **e)** angel **[5]**
2. **a)** ferries **b)** lilies **c)** jellies **d)** cherries **[4]**
3. **a)** clapping **b)** patting **c)** wrapping
   d) dropping **e)** hopping **f)** humming **[6]**
4. **a)** knitting **b)** knuckle **c)** knock **d)** knee **[4]**
5. **a)** fatter, fattest **b)** sadder, saddest
   c) runnier, runniest **[6]**
6. wriggle, wrapper, writing **[3]**
7. **a)** city **b)** fancy **c)** face **d)** cell **[4]**
8. **a)** excitement **b)** playful
   c) careful (accept careless) **[3]**

Pages 60–61

Challenge 1

1.

'or' spelling pronounced er after 'w'		'ar' spelling pronounced or after 'w'	
word	work	war	towards
worm	worse	warm	warn

[8]

Challenge 2

1. **a)** working **b)** warning **c)** warmed **[3]**

Challenge 3

1. **a)** ward **b)** wardrobe
   c) war **d)** dwarf **[4]**

Pages 62–63

Challenge 1

1. flowerpot/plantpot, bedroom, teaspoon, football, eyebrow, armchair **[6]**

Challenge 2

1. **a)** wardrobe **b)** toenail
   c) carpark **d)** handbag/handball **[4]**

Challenge 3

1. **a)** teacup, windowsill
   b) strawberry, breakfast
   c) newspaper, bookshelf
   d) bumblebee, rosebush **[8]**

Pages 64–65

Challenge 1

1. **a)** must not **b)** did not **c)** should not
   d) has not **e)** could not **f)** have not **[6]**

Challenge 2

1. **a)** aren't **b)** They're **c)** She's **d)** there's **[4]**

Challenge 3

1. **a)** we're **b)** he's **c)** he'd **d)** I'll **[4]**

Pages 66–67

Challenge 1

1. **a)** the lady's gloves **b)** Nadia's bike
   c) Mum's car **[3]**

Challenge 2

1. **a)** The cat is sleeping in the **dog's** bed.
   b) There is a **bird's** nest at the top of the tree.
   c) Mum stood on **Dad's** toe.
   d) **Joe's** shoes are muddy. **[4]**

Challenge 3

1.

Apostrophe to show a contraction	Apostrophe to show possession
isn't Freddie's	Jaz's sums The dog's paw

[4]

Pages 68–69

Challenge 1

1. **a)** too **b)** two **c)** sea **d)** see
   e) blew **f)** blue **[6]**

Challenge 2

1. **a)** peas **b)** quiet **c)** won **[3]**

Challenge 3

1. knew, there, would, be, to **[5]**

Pages 70–71

Challenge 1

1. Words spelt correctly. **[9]**

Challenge 2

1. Answers will vary. Examples: palm, half. **[2]**
2. Answers will vary. Examples: steak, break **[2]**

Challenge 3

1. Answers will vary. Example: **W**ill **a**nd **T**ina **e**njoy **r**unning. **[1]**

Pages 72–75

1. **a)** flying **b)** copied **c)** replied **d)** crying **[4]**
2. **a)** the strong bodies **b)** the little ponies
   c) the marching armies **d)** the red cherries **[4]**
3. **a)** wart **b)** warm **c)** swarm **[3]**
4. **a)** petal **b)** pencil **c)** plural **d)** tunnel **[4]**
5. **a)** won't **b)** there's **c)** can't
   d) should've **e)** she'd **[5]**
6. **a)** warned **b)** warmer **c)** working **[3]**
7. **a)** tidily **b)** messily **c)** crazily **[3]**
8. **a)** night **b)** flour **c)** hare **[3]**

Fill in your score for each progress test in the window of the rocket.